STEP ONE:

Play Recorder

by Gerald Burakoff

**Master the basics as you step into the exciting world of playing the recorder.
A complete and proven method that includes over fifty classical and folk tunes
to play and enjoy as you learn.**

Cover photography by Randall Wallace

Order No. AM 945604
US International Standard Book Number: 0.8256.1645.X
UK International Standard Book Number: 0.7119.6763.6

Exclusive Distributors:
Music Sales Corporation
257 Park Avenue South, New York, NY 10010 USA
Music Sales Limited
8/9 Frith Street, London W1V 5TZ England
Music Sales Pty. Limited
120 Rothschild Street, Rosebery, Sydney, NSW 2018, Australia

Printed in the United States of America by
Vicks Lithograph and Printing Corporation

Amsco Publications
New York/London/Sydney

CD Track List

Contents

Recorder Basics

The recorder is a vertical flute with a beak-shaped mouthpiece into which a block *(fipple)* is inserted to form the windway.

Recorder Range

Most recorders today are patterned after instruments of the Baroque period. They have a full chromatic range of two octaves and a minor third, and a strong, reedy tone quality.

The soprano recorder sounds one octave higher than notated, and its range is

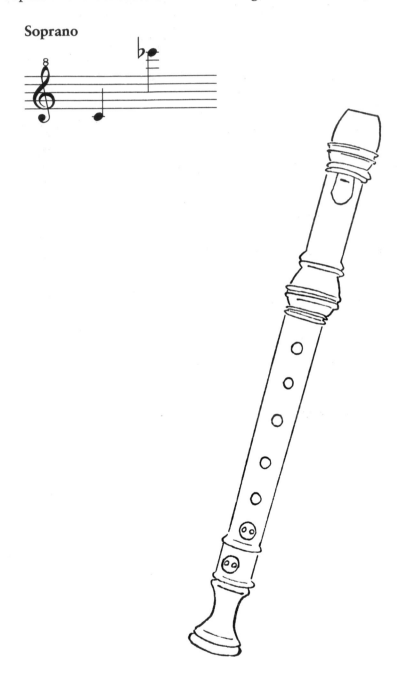

Soprano

Recorder Fingering (English and German)

The great majority of recorders are now made with either English (baroque) or German fingering systems. The major difference between English-fingered and German-fingered recorders is in the fingering for F and F♯ on the C instruments (soprano, tenor, great bass) and B♭ and B on F instruments (sopranino, alto, bass). English-fingered recorders require a forked fingering for these notes; German-fingered instruments do not. There is an external difference between the two recorders: The English-fingered instrument has a small fourth and a large fifth hole while the German-fingered instrument has a large fourth and a small fifth hole.

Recorder Care

Both wooden and plastic instruments need delicate, although different, care if they are to last, and remain in excellent playing condition.

Wooden Recorders:

1. Play the instrument only at room temperature. This can be achieved by holding the instrument under the armpit before playing.

2. After each playing session the recorder should be taken apart and dried with a swab.

3. Break in a new instrument gradually: twenty minutes at a time for the first two weeks, and thirty minutes for approximately the next two weeks.

4. Do not expose the recorder to extreme temperature changes.

5. Use cork grease for easier assembly of the instrument, and to avoid drying out the corks .

6. Oil the bore lightly approximately every six months.

Plastic Recorders:

1. Play the instrument only at room temperature. This can be achieved by holding the instrument under the armpit before playing.

2. After playing, dry the interior of the instrument with a swab.

3. Wipe the exterior with a lint-free cloth.

4. The recorder should be washed occasionally with a mild, gentle soap in warm water, rinsed, and dried.

Recorder Technique

1. Hold the recorder with the left hand on top and the right hand at the bottom.

2. Place the recorder between the lips and in front of the teeth.

3. Cover the thumb-hole with the left thumb at a 45° angle to the recorder. This step is extremely important, because an incorrect thumb position causes a poor hand position.

4. Keeping the thumb-hole covered, cover the first hole at the top with the first finger of the left hand. Recorder holes should be covered with the cushions (pads) of the fingers.

5. No finger pressure is necessary.

6. Rest the recorder on the right thumb, between the fourth and fifth holes.

7. Fingers which are not being used at this stage should remain slightly above but not touching the holes.

8. Bring the corners of the mouth gently and slightly forward.

9. Exhale gently into the recorder and think of making a silent "daah" sound.

10. Always play softly and tongue (silent "daah") gently.

11. The lips and fingers should be relaxed at all times.

12. Tongue every note. Do not slur from note to note.

Playing the Recorder

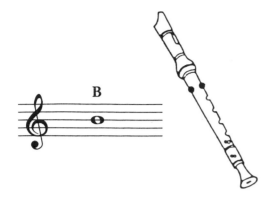

In $\frac{4}{4}$ meter there are four beats in each measure, and a quarter note ($\quarternote$) receives a beat. A quarter rest $\quarterrest$; receives one beat of silence.

The B Note

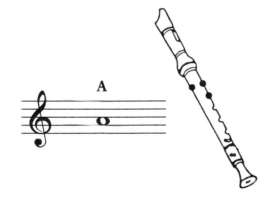

The A Note

B and A Notes

8

A half note (♩) receives two beats.
A half rest (–) receives two beats of silence.

Half Notes and Half Rests

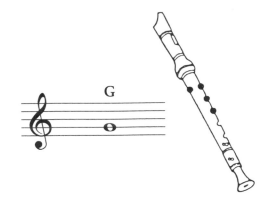

The G Note

Half Notes and Quarter Notes

Au Claire de la Lune

French

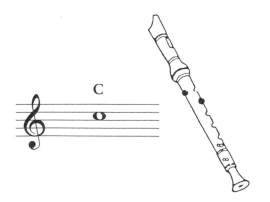

In $\frac{2}{4}$ meter there are two beats in each measure, and a quarter note ($\quarternote$) receives one beat.

The C Note

Paris

French

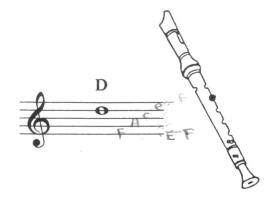

In ¾ meter there are three beats in each measure, and a quarter note (♩) receives one beat. A half note receives two beats, and a dotted half note (♩.) receives three beats.

In May

German

An incomplete measure occurs when the music does not begin on the first beat. The missing beats are found in the last measure of music.

Folk Song

German

A whole note (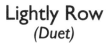) receives four beats.
A whole rest (–) receives one full measure of silence.

Lightly Row
(Duet)

German

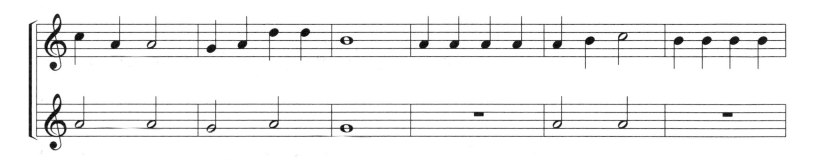

Fais Do-Do

French

Waltz Song

German

An eighth note (♪) is equal to ½ of a quarter note. Two eighth notes (♫) are equal to one quarter note. An eighth rest (𝄾) receives ½ a beat of silence.

Go From My Window

English

Winter, Goodbye!

German

Hop Dance

German

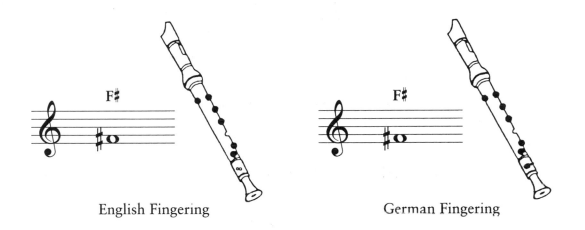

English Fingering   German Fingering

A sharp (♯) raises the pitch of a note by one half-step. When a sharp is written before the note F the note becomes F-sharp.

Hymn Tune

German

(same as 4/4 meter)

Holiday Song

Polish

A sharp (♯) placed on the fifth line of the staff, after the clef sign, is called a key signature.
Every F in the music must be played as F-sharp.

Dance Song

German

Staccato (♩ ⸌) means to play notes short and detached.
Tenuto (♩ ⸌) means to play notes for their fullest values.

Mice and Crickets

Austrian

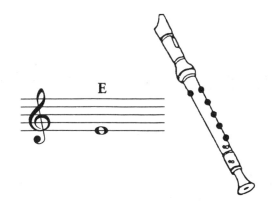

Folk Tune

Welsh

A repeat sign (:‖) means to repeat from the beginning, or from the previous reversed repeat sign (‖:).

Evening Melody

Swedish

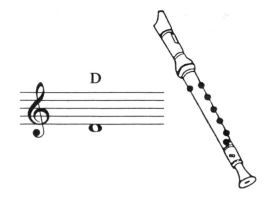

Good King Wenceslas

Bohemian

A fermata ($\frown$) above a note means to hold the note a little longer than written.

Flow Gently, Sweet Afton

Scottish

Ritard or *rit.* means to slow down—gradually.

Grandfather's Clock

American

Da Capo, D.C.—from the beginning.
Fine—the end.
D.C. al Fine—go back to the beginning of the music and play to the end.

Minuet

Bach

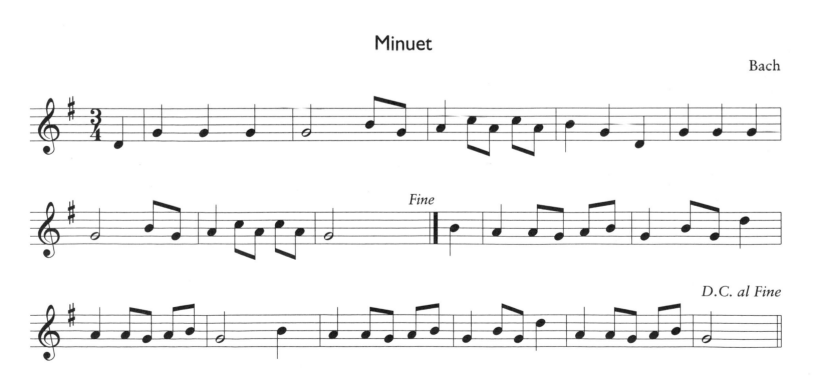

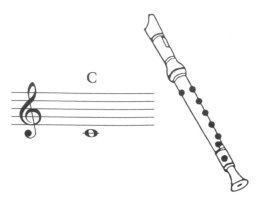

C

Tideo

American

Tempo marks indicate how fast or slow to play the music.

The Old Man

Scottish

Allegro(fast)

English Fingering   German Fingering

Blow the Man Down

Sea chantey

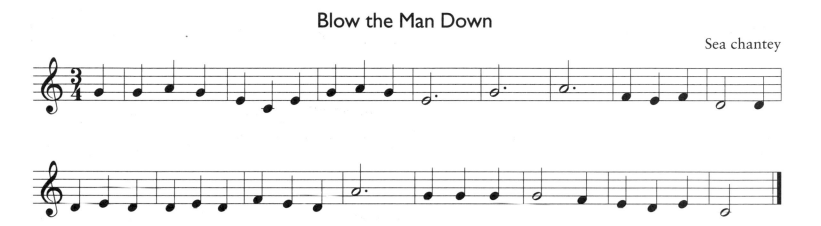

In a round the same melody is played by two or more people starting at different times.

Oh, How Lovely Is the Evening
(Round)

German

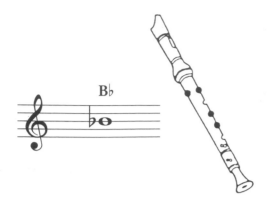

A flat (♭) lowers the pitch of a note by one half-step. A flat (♭) placed on the third line of the staff, after the clef sign, is called the key signature. Every B in the music must be played as B-flat.

Scarborough Fair

English

The Nightingale

French

Moderato (moderately)

A dot after a note receives ½ the value of that note. One dotted quarter note and one eighth note together (♩. ♪) make up two beats.

The Streets of Laredo

American

Over the Hills and Far Away

English

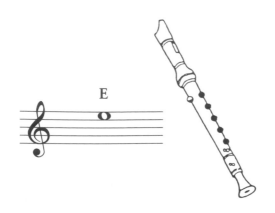

E

Rigaudon

Daquin

Allegretto (moderately fast)

Must I Then?

German

Fine

D.C. al Fine

Auld Lang Syne

Scottish

My Country, 'Tis of Thee

English

Frère Jacques
(Round)

French

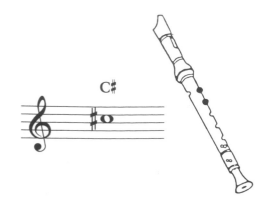

C#

America, the Beautiful

American

Come, Ye Thankful People
(Duet)

Hymn tune

Learn both parts of this duet.

Recorder 1

Recorder 2

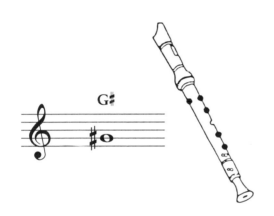

G#

The Blues Bells of Scotland

Scottish

A tie (♩‿♩) connects two notes of the same pitch. The notes are played as one, and are held for the total.

Yankee Doodle Boy

G. Cohan

Coventry Carol

English

Andante (moderately slow)

Dreydel

Holiday Song

Allegro

In ⅔ meter there are two beats in each measure, and a half note (♩) receives one beat. This meter can also be indicated with the symbol ₵, and is called *cut time*.

St. Paul's Steeple

English

When the Saints Go Marching In

American

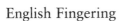

English Fingering

German Fingering

Duke Street

Hymn

The Marines' Hymn

Traditional
Fine

D.C. al Fine

First and *second ending signs* mean: Play from the beginning to the repeat sign (:‖) in the first ending. Then return to the beginning or to the sign (‖:) and play the section again. This time, skip the first ending and go to the second ending.

Vive la Compagnie

French-Canadian

In § meter there are six beats in each measure, and an eighth note (♪) receives one beat.

Oh Dear, What Can the Matter Be?

English

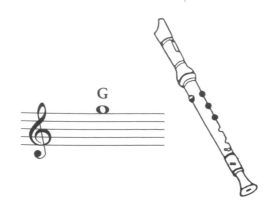

G

Waltz

German

Allegretto

Gavotte

M. Praetorius

Moderato

Fingering Chart

◯ open hole

● closed hole

◐ partly open hole

*This fingering is for double hole recorders. Single hole recorders must be covered like this ◖

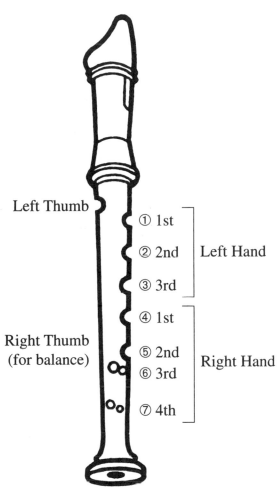

Left Thumb

① 1st
② 2nd   Left Hand
③ 3rd

Right Thumb
(for balance)

④ 1st
⑤ 2nd   Right Hand
⑥ 3rd
⑦ 4th

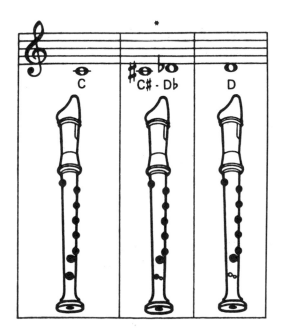

C   C# - Db   D

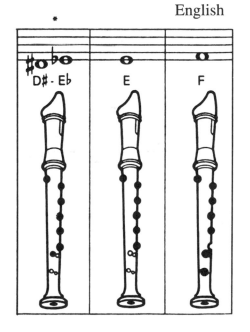

English

D# - Eb   E   F

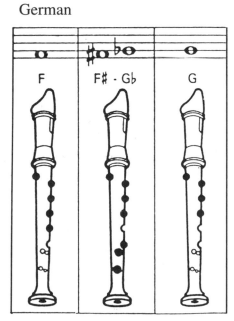

German

F   F# - Gb   G

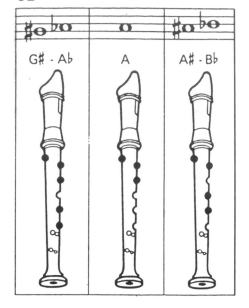

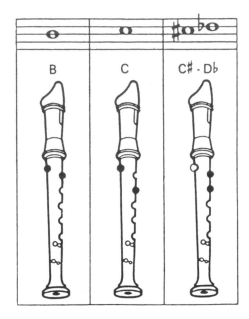

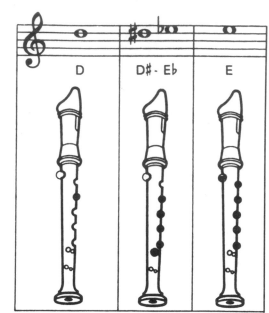

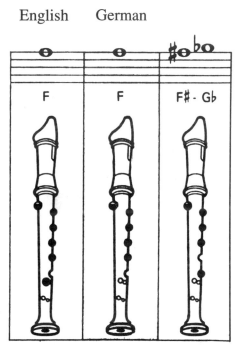

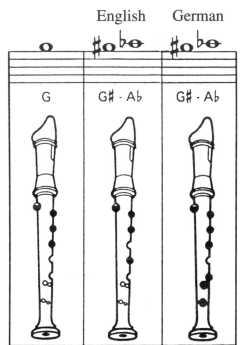

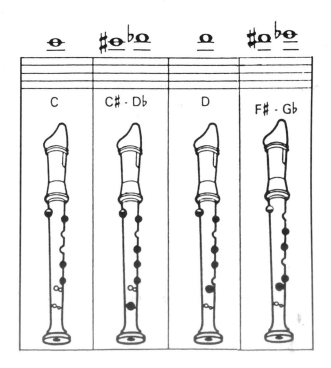